the soy sauce cookbook

the SOY sauce cookbook

Explore the flavour-enhancing
power of Asia's magic
ingredient

APPLE

by Jenny Stacey and
Maureen Keller

A QUINTET BOOK

Published by Apple Press
6 Blundell Street
London N7 9BH

ISBN 1-84092-240-0

This book was designed and produced by
Quintet Publishing Limited
6 Blundell Street
London N7 9BH

creative director: **Richard Dewing**
art director: **Clare Reynolds.**
design: **Balley Design Associates**
designers: **Simon Balley & Joanna Hill**
project editor: **Doreen Palamartschuk**
editor: **Jane Hurd-Cosgrave**
photographer: **David Armstrong**

Typeset in Great Britain by
Central Southern Typesetters, Eastbourne
Manufactured in Singapore by
United Graphic Pte Ltd
Printed in Singapore by
Star Standard Industries Pte Ltd
Photographs on pages 6(tl), 7, 8(bl), and 9(tr)
courtesy of Kikkoman Soy Sauce.

Known as *Shoyu* or "fermented savory agent" in Japan and *jiang yong* in China, soy sauce is as indispensable to cooks and chefs in China and Japan as salt, pepper, and mustard are elsewhere. It is an essential component of all Asian cooking. Every table hosts a bottle of light or dark soy sauce at all mealtimes to be used as a seasoning or dip.

We still associate soy sauce with Asian recipes and cooking methods, and do not use it to its full potential. In fact, soy sauce is a healthy, versatile ingredient that can be used as a basis for rich sauces, broths, dips, marinades, and salad dressings, or simply drizzled over roast or fried dishes, enhancing everything it touches with its uniquely piquant flavor.

above: **A traditional soy sauce ceramic jar.**

light and dark soy sauce

Although there are a few variations with additional ingredients for added flavor, the two main types of soy sauce are the light and the dark varieties. These are each very distinctive, and each blend best with different types of food.

Light soy sauce, as the name implies, is light in color and less powerful in flavor, although the flavor remains full. It is more widely used for sauces, and is the most suitable for use in cooking. Saltier than dark soy sauce, it is known in Asian stores as Superior Soy, and is mainly used in soups or with fish, seafood, light meats, and poultry.

Dark soy sauce is matured for a longer period than light soy, which causes its dark, almost-black appearance. Slightly thicker than light soy, it has a stronger, sweeter flavor, and is more suitable for stews, casseroles, and recipes with dark meats. It is also used when a dipping sauce consisting only of soy sauce is called for. It is known to Asian grocers as Soy Superior Sauce.

below: **Dark soy sauce.**

what is soy sauce?

Called "liquid spice," naturally brewed soy sauce contains more than 280 aromatic ingredients, including vanilla extract, fruits, flowers, meat, fish, and alcohol, which enable it to enhance many dishes with its subtle fragrance. Based on soybeans, wheat, water, salt, and a specially developed yeast, soy sauce is brewed in a similar fashion to a fine wine. Other ingredients are added according to the origin of the sauce. Pork is added in Canton; ginger and mushrooms are added in Peking; occasionally, anchovy paste is also added. Naturally brewed soy sauce is free from additives and preservatives. There are, however, other less-natural processes that are used to produce soy sauce chemically. These are considered to be inferior in aroma and flavor by true soy-sauce connoisseurs.

the history of soy sauce

Japanese soy sauce was first introduced to the West by Dutch explorers in the 17th century. It was they who introduced it to Europe, exporting it in stone jars and barrels. Soy sauce soon became popular in France, where Louis XIV's royal chefs discovered its uses as a flavor enhancer.

above: **The Imperial Soy Sauce Museum, Goyogura, Japan.**

The Chinese, however, were the original users of soy sauce. They introduced it to Japan, along with the influence of Buddhism, over 1,500 years ago. The Buddhist religion forbade the use of meat- and fish-based sauces, which traditionally played a great part in flavoring foods. Soy sauce soon became a popular seasoning in Japan, although it was changed from its original form—it was originally made only from soybeans, and the Japanese version had wheat added to it.

how soy sauce is produced

Naturally brewed soy sauce is produced when soybeans and wheat are mixed together to form a dry mash known as "koji." The koji mixture grows over a period of 45 hours, during which time special enzymes that are vital to the sauce's final flavor, color, and aroma begin to form. Next, a salt-water solution is added, and the mixture is then left to ferment for up to six months. The resulting mixture is known as a "mature

below: **Ancient Japanese soy sauce production drawing.**

mash," and resembles a smooth, reddish-brown liquid. The mash is then pressed between layers of cloth to extract the clear soy sauce, which is then pasteurized and bottled.

A good soy sauce has 280 different flavor and aroma components. These blend in such a way that no single flavor dominates, resulting in a product that may be used with a wide variety of ingredients. There are three methods of producing soy sauce, and the end products vary in quality and flavor: one type of fermented or brewed soy sauce is produced by fermenting the soy beans, wheat, water, and salt with no further additions. This type is completely natural.

A non-brewed sauce is chemically produced by hydrolyzing plant protein, which is then blended with colorings, salt water, corn syrup, and caramel.

A semi-brewed soy sauce is also produced by combining the two previous methods together. Artificial or chemically produced soy sauce is made when the vegetable or plant proteins are decomposed at a high temperature by the addition of powerful acids, such as hydrochloric acid. This mixture is then neutralized with the addition of soda. The final additions are HVP (hydrolyzed vegetable protein), sugar, salt, and caramel. The final product is considered to be lacking in flavor and aroma when compared to naturally brewed soy sauces, such as Japanese brands.

Chinese-style soy sauce is different again. This ferments in just 30 days. The lack of yeast gives a fermentation that is low in alcohol and lactic acids, and a resultant sauce that some people say lacks flavor and aroma.

Japanese-style, naturally brewed soy sauce is made by traditional methods that have been handed down for 350 years. The soy beans are first steamed, and then mixed with equal proportions of roasted, crushed-wheat kernels. Yeast is then added to start the natural-fermentation process. After three days, the soy and wheat-germ mixture grows a mold over the surface, at which stage it is known as

above: **Light soy sauce.**

below: **Drawing of Japanese soy sauce production.**

"koji." This mixture is blended with salted water, and the resulting wet mash is put into fermentation tanks.

Over a period of weeks, the soybean protein changes to amino acids, which give the final sauce its characteristic taste. Wheat starch changes to sugar, and the mixture of this and the acids forms the color of the sauce. The sugar content gradually changes to alcohol, and some of the alcohol and sugar transforms into various acids, which add tartness to the flavor. This mixture is left to mature for six months, and then pressed. The liquid, which is the soy sauce, is then drawn off, pasteurized, and bottled.

above: **Soy fermenting in chrysanthemum-wood vats.**

soy sauce today

You can see from these different processes that there are different qualities of soy sauce on the market today. If possible, try to use the naturally brewed sauces in your cooking to give a fuller flavor.

There is an ancient taste-test that is said to distinguish between a good sauce and a lesser sauce: a good sauce can be enjoyed on its own when poured into a small dish, but a lesser sauce will be too harsh and unpleasant if used in this way.

Soy sauce was initially used as a seasoning by the Chinese to complement their vegetarian diet; now, it is also used in stewed dishes and marinades in China, and as a table condiment in Indonesia. It may be used in many types of cooking—not all of them Asian—and with many ingredients. The addition of soy sauce gives a spicy, salty flavor to dishes, without overpowering them. Soy sauce is generally used in small quantities, as you will see from the following recipes.

Another advantage of soy sauce as a condiment and flavor-enhancer is that it has an indefinite shelf-life if stored correctly, and so does not need to be used quickly. Store the sauce as you would a fine wine, with its cap firmly sealed, and keep it in the refrigerator or a cool place to prevent it from oxidizing. Once you begin to realize the full potential of soy sauce by trying the delicious recipes featured in this book, long storage will not be an issue you will have to consider. So get out the soy sauce, and enter a whole new world of tastes!

below: **A modern collection of soy sauce bottles.**

savory
snacks

Curried Parcels

Easy to prepare, these parcels may be served hot or cold, perhaps with a mint-and-yogurt dip to complement the Indian flavors in the filling.

serves 4

3 oz prepared puff pastry, thawed	1 tsp garam masala
1 egg, beaten	½ tsp chili powder
1 tsp sesame seeds	1 Tbsp peach chutney
	2 tsp lemon juice
	1 small carrot, finely
for the filling	diced
1 Tbsp butter	1 Tbsp light soy sauce
2 scallions, chopped	¾ cup diced, cooked
2 garlic cloves, minced	potato

Melt the butter for the filling, and gently cook the scallions, garlic, garam masala, chili, chutney, lemon juice, carrot, and soy sauce, stirring for 3 to 4 minutes. Add the potato, mix well, and let cool completely.

Heat the oven to 400°F. Roll the pastry out into an 8-inch square. Cut into four 4-inch squares. Brush the edges of the squares with beaten egg, and place a little filling in the center of each square. Carefully draw the corners to the center to form a parcel, sealing the seams by pressing together. Repeat with all of the squares.

Place the parcels on a dampened baking sheet, brush with beaten egg, and sprinkle with the sesame seeds. Bake in the oven until golden, about 15 minutes.

Stuffed Mushrooms

Capers, feta cheese, and soy sauce give these stuffed mushrooms a
Middle Eastern flavor.

makes 14 to 16 mushrooms

¾ lb large mushrooms (14 to 16)

¼ cup crumbled feta cheese

¼ cup Italian-style bread crumbs

½ tsp olive oil (plus oil for brushing the mushrooms)

1 tsp light soy sauce

½ tsp ground thyme

1 tsp grated onion

3 tsp capers, drained

Wash the mushrooms and remove the stems. Chop the stems very finely
and place in a bowl. Add 3 tablespoons of the cheese, together with the
bread crumbs, and mix thoroughly. Stir in the olive oil and soy sauce.
When well blended, stir in the thyme, grated onion, and drained capers.

Brush the mushroom caps with olive oil, inside and out. Stuff with the
bread-crumb mixture. Then crumble the remaining tablespoon of feta over
the mushrooms. Broil until heated thoroughly, and the tops have begun to
brown, about 6 to 8 minutes.

Spicy Peanuts

Plain peanuts make a good appetizer, but spicy peanuts are even better. Use a hot curry powder, and serve them with lots of beer.

makes 1 lb

1 Tbsp olive oil	1 Tbsp light soy sauce
2 large garlic cloves, minced	1 Tbsp Worcestershire sauce
1 lb roasted, unsalted peanuts	1 tsp curry powder

Heat the olive oil in a pan, and add the garlic, stirring. Add the peanuts, soy sauce, Worcestershire sauce, and curry powder. Sauté for a few minutes until the liquid has been absorbed. Remove peanuts from the heat, and cool before serving.

Hot-and-Spicy Chicken Wings

A real favorite for supper, these chicken wings are also perfect for barbecues.

serves 4

2 lb chicken wings	A few drops of Tabasco sauce
2 Tbsp garlic-wine vinegar	1 Tbsp tomato paste
2 Tbsp honey	⅔ cup strained tomatoes
1 Tbsp Worcestershire sauce	1 tsp prepared mustard
2 Tbsp dark soy sauce	

Heat the oven to 350°F. Place the chicken wings in a shallow, ovenproof dish. Place the vinegar, honey, Worcestershire sauce, soy sauce, Tabasco sauce, tomato paste, strained tomatoes, and mustard in a bowl. Mix well. Pour over the chicken wings, turning to coat evenly.

Cook the chicken wings in the oven until cooked through, about 45 minutes. Serve hot with salad.

Fried Shrimp Rolls

These Asian-style shrimp-filled bites are delicious, with their complementary hints of coconut and lime. Prepare them in advance, then store in the refrigerator so they will be ready to cook just before serving.

serves 4

4 thick slices of white bread, with crusts removed
1 Tbsp butter, softened
1 Tbsp all-purpose flour
2 Tbsp coconut milk
1 Tbsp light soy sauce
1 Tbsp Romano cheese, shredded
Grated rind of 1 lime
½ cup peeled, cooked shrimp, chopped
2 scallions, finely chopped
Ground black pepper

Oil for deep frying
1 cup fresh, brown-bread crumbs
1 Tbsp sesame seeds
1 egg, beaten

for the dip
⅔ cup yogurt
⅔ cup mayonnaise
1 tsp fish sauce
1 Tbsp tomato paste
1 tsp lime juice
1 Tbsp chopped, fresh parsley

Using a rolling pin, flatten the bread slices until very thin. Melt the butter in a pan, add the flour, and mix well. Cook for 1 minute, then add the coconut milk and bring to a boil, stirring. Remove the pan from the heat and stir in the soy sauce, cheese, lime rind, shrimp, and scallions. Season with pepper.

Spread the mixture onto the bread, roll up, and cut each slice into four. Mix the ingredients for the dip, and chill until required.

Heat the oil in a wok or frying pan to 370°F. Meanwhile, mix the brown-bread crumbs and sesame seeds together in a bowl. Then place the beaten egg in a separate bowl. Dip each piece into the egg and then roll in the bread-crumb mixture to coat completely. Fry in the hot oil for 3 minutes. Drain on paper towels to remove excess oil, and serve with the dip.

Sesame Pikelets

Pikelets are a traditional form of pancake. Make the batter just before cooking.
It is thicker than normal pancake batter, in order to hold its shape in the pan.

serves 4

for the pikelets	for the topping
1 cup self-rising flour	8 oz smoked-salmon
1 tsp sesame seeds	fillets
2 Tbsp butter, melted	2 Tbsp snipped, fresh
(plus extra for	chives
frying)	1 Tbsp chopped dill
⅔ cup milk	⅔ cup sour cream
1 Tbsp light soy sauce	Lemon wedges

Sift the flour into a large mixing bowl. Add the sesame seeds and make a well in the center, gradually whisking in the butter, milk, and soy sauce.

Grease a large, heavy-based frying pan or wok with butter. Drop 2 tablespoons of mixture into the pan for each pikelet, cooking two at a time. Cook until the surface of the pikelet bubbles, and then turn them until each side is browned, about 2 to 3 minutes. Cool on a rack. Repeat until all the mixture is used.

Slice the smoked salmon. Mix half of the herbs into the sour cream. Spoon the sour cream onto the pikelets, top with the salmon, and sprinkle with the remaining herbs. Top with lemon wedges, and serve with a small salad.

Hot-and-Sour Shrimp Soup

This really is a colorful soup in all aspects. Filled with shrimp and vegetables, it has a truly unique flavor.

serves 4

4 dried Chinese mushrooms

3¾ cups vegetable stock

I cup peeled, cooked shrimp

¾ cup sliced, pickled Asian vegetables

½ cup canned bamboo shoots, drained and sliced

3 scallions, sliced

I zucchini, shredded

½-inch piece fresh gingerroot, shredded

2 tomatoes, seeded and diced

2 tsp rice wine or sherry

2 Tbsp light soy sauce

I Tbsp red-wine vinegar

2 Tbsp diced, smoked ham

I tsp sesame oil

Soak the dried mushrooms in warm water for 20 minutes. Squeeze dry, remove the stems, and slice. Bring the stock to a boil in a large saucepan. Add the shrimp, vegetables, bamboo shoots, scallions, zucchini, ginger, and tomatoes. Simmer for 5 minutes.

Add the rice wine or sherry, soy sauce, vinegar, and ham. Cook for I minute, then stir in the sesame oil. Serve immediately.

Marinated Mushroom Caps

These tasty mushrooms get better the longer they marinate. They are delicious whole, but also can be sliced and added to liven up salads.

serves 6

2 cups fresh, white mushrooms

2 Tbsp light soy sauce

¼ cup red wine (Merlot is recommended)

2 Tbsp red-wine vinegar

I Tbsp sugar

Remove and discard stems from the mushrooms. Wash the caps and pat them dry. Place the caps in a bowl or jar with a tight lid. Mix the soy sauce, wine, vinegar, and sugar together. Pour over the mushroom caps.

Marinate the mushrooms in the refrigerator at least overnight or up to three days, turning occasionally. Serve in a bowl with toothpicks.

Vegetable Beignets

Crisp vegetables fried in a light batter, which lets the true colors of the vegetables be seen, make an attractive and delicious appetizer.

serves 4

¾ lb mixed vegetables, such as asparagus spears, peppers, snow peas, cauliflower, and broccoli

Oil for deep frying

for the sauce
I red chile, chopped
4 Tbsp light soy sauce
4 Tbsp vermouth
⅓ cup strained tomatoes

¼ cup vegetable broth
I Tbsp firmly packed brown sugar

for the batter
I egg
⅔ cup water
I Tbsp light soy sauce
I cup all-purpose flour
½ cup cornstarch
Dash of salt

Blanch the vegetables for 3 minutes, then drain well and pat dry with paper towels. Mix the sauce ingredients together. Place in a small pan, and heat gently until the sugar dissolves. Keep warm.

Beat the egg, water, and soy sauce for the batter. Sift the flour, cornstarch, and salt into a bowl. Make a well in the center and gradually whisk in the egg mixture to form a smooth batter.

Heat the oil to 370°F in a wok. Dip the vegetables into the batter, then deep-fry in the oil for 2 to 3 minutes. Remove with a slotted spoon and drain on paper towels. Serve with the dipping sauce.

Pork Spareribs

These delicious ribs are cooked in a wok with a spicy barbecue sauce.

serves 4

1½ lb country-style pork ribs, cut into 2-inch pieces	1 tsp ground ginger
2 Tbsp vegetable oil	2 garlic cloves, finely diced
3 Tbsp dark soy sauce	¼ tsp Chinese five-spice powder
3 Tbsp honey	3 Tbsp red-wine vinegar
2 Tbsp Worcestershire sauce	3 oz firmly packed dark-brown sugar
⅔ cup strained tomatoes	2 Tbsp lime juice

Prepare the ribs and heat the oil in a wok. Add the ribs and cook until brown, about 5 minutes. Reduce heat and cook for a further 10 minutes. Place all the remaining ingredients in a saucepan, and heat gently to dissolve the sugar.

Pour the sauce into the wok with the ribs. Cover and cook until the ribs are cooked well throughout, about 30 minutes. Serve.

Country Pâté

This pâté is lighter than most meat pâtés since it is made with chicken and pork.

serves 8

1¼ cups chicken breast, diced	1 tsp cumin seeds
1 cup pork slices, diced	2 tsp mixed peppercorns
⅔ cup smoked bacon, finely diced	5 Tbsp brandy
½ tsp salt	2 Tbsp light soy sauce
½ tsp ground nutmeg	Hot toast or bread to serve
2 garlic cloves, diced	

Lightly grease a two-pound loaf pan. Place the chicken, pork, and bacon in a large mixing bowl. Add the salt, nutmeg, garlic, and cumin. Crush the peppercorns, and add these to the mixture with the brandy and soy sauce. Mix very well, cover, and let sit for at least 1 hour.

Heat the oven to 300°F. Spoon the mixture into the loaf pan, pressing down well. Place in a roasting pan half filled with hot water. Cook the pâté in the oven about 1½ to 1¾ hours. Remove from the water and let cool. Unmold the pâté, slice, and serve with hot toast or bread.

Salmon Paté

This is a really speedy-yet-delicious appetizer. Once the fish is cooked, all the ingredients are simply blended in a food processor. For extra speed, use canned salmon.

serves 4

1 8-oz salmon fillet	1 Tbsp capers
½ cup cream cheese	Ground black pepper
1 Tbsp light soy sauce	½ tsp paprika
1 Tbsp chopped, fresh dill	Dill sprigs and lemon slices, to garnish
1 Tbsp chopped, fresh parsley	Hot toast triangles, to serve
1 Tbsp lemon juice	

Poach the salmon fillets in a large, shallow pan for 8 to 10 minutes or until cooked through. Remove from the pan, drain, and skin the fish. Chop the fish into pieces and let cool completely.

Place the cream cheese, soy sauce, dill, parsley, lemon juice, capers, pepper, and cooked salmon in a food processor, and blend 15 seconds.

Transfer to four individual-serving ramekins or small dishes. Sprinkle with paprika and chill until required. Garnish with the dill and lemon, and serve with hot toast triangles.

poultry with pizzazz

Honeyed Chicken Breasts

This honey-and-ginger sauce has a wonderful taste and aroma, and complements the poultry perfectly. Try using turkey as a substitute for chicken for an equally delicious dish.

serves 4

1 Tbsp vegetable oil	4 Tbsp honey
2 Tbsp butter	1 cup chicken broth
4 half chicken breasts, boned	2 Tbsp light soy sauce
1 garlic clove, minced	3 pieces preserved stem ginger, sliced
2 leeks, sliced	2 Tbsp syrup from preserved ginger jar
1 red bell pepper, cut into strips	2 Tbsp garlic wine vinegar
½ cup baby corn, halved lengthwise	2 Tbsp cornstarch
2 Tbsp firmly packed brown sugar	

Heat the oil and butter in a frying pan or wok until the butter has melted. Add the chicken and cook for 5 minutes, turning. Add the garlic and leeks, and cook for a further 3 minutes. Stir in the red pepper, baby corn, sugar, honey, broth, soy sauce, stem ginger, ginger syrup, and vinegar.

Reduce the heat to a simmer and cook until the chicken is cooked well through, about 20 minutes. Blend the cornstarch with 4 tablespoons of cold water, and stir into the pan. Bring to a boil, and cook until the sauce is thickened and clear. Cook for a further 2 minutes and serve.

Chicken in Black-Bean Sauce

This sauce is easy to make, and far superior to the bottled sauce you can buy.

serves 4	
1 cup vegetable oil	1/2 cup snow peas
12 oz boned chicken	2 Tbsp canned black
breast, cut into	beans, washed
strips	1/2-inch piece fresh
1 cup oyster mushrooms	gingerroot, shredded
1 small yellow bell	1 garlic clove, minced
pepper, diced	2 Tbsp sherry
1 small green bell	1 cup chicken broth
pepper, diced	2 Tbsp light soy sauce
6 scallions, chopped	2 Tbsp cornstarch

Heat the oil in a wok and cook the chicken for 3 minutes. Using a slotted spoon, remove the chicken from the oil, and drain on paper towels. Pour the oil from the wok, leaving 3 tablespoons. Add the mushrooms, peppers, scallions, and snow peas to the wok, and stir-fry for 3 minutes.

Mash the black beans with the ginger, garlic, and sherry in a bowl. Add to the wok, and then stir in the chicken broth and soy sauce. Cook for 3 minutes. Blend the cornstarch with 4 tablespoons of cold water to make a paste, and then stir into the wok. Bring to a boil, add the chicken, and cook for 5 minutes, stirring. Serve.

Chicken with Mustard Sauce

Wholegrain mustard is used here for a strong flavor with added texture.

serves 4	
1 Tbsp vegetable oil	2 1/2 cups open-cap
2 garlic cloves, minced	mushrooms, sliced
1 lb chicken breast,	2 Tbsp wholegrain
boned and skinned	mustard
1 fennel bulb, trimmed	3 Tbsp chopped, fresh
2 Tbsp light soy sauce	chives
1/2 stick butter	Salt and ground black
2/3 cup heavy cream	pepper

Heat the oil in a large frying pan or wok and cook the garlic for 1 minute. Cut the chicken into 1-inch cubes, add to the pan, and cook for 2 to 3 minutes, stirring. Add the sliced fennel, soy sauce, and butter, and stir-fry for 5 minutes. Stir in the cream, mushrooms, and mustard, and cook for 5 minutes. Sprinkle with chopped chives. Season and serve.

Asian Cashew Casserole

Soy sauce is excellent in casseroles, its piquancy adding a hint of Asia to this cashew nut and chicken dish.

serves 4

2 Tbsp sunflower oil	½ cup unsalted cashew
4 chicken pieces	nuts
8 shallots	1 Tbsp tomato paste
2 cups chestnut	Salt and ground black
mushrooms,	pepper
quartered	
1 cup baby turnips	for the
2 celery stalks, sliced	dumplings
1 carrot, diced	1 cup self-rising flour
¼ cup all-purpose flour	½ cup shredded beef
2½ cups chicken broth	suet
2 Tbsp light soy sauce	1 Tbsp light soy sauce
⅔ cup dry white wine	1 Tbsp chopped, fresh
	rosemary

Heat the oil in a large frying pan or wok. Add the chicken and cook until browned, about 10 minutes. Remove with a slotted spoon, and place in an ovenproof casserole dish. Heat the oven to 350°F. Add the shallots, mushrooms, turnips, celery, and carrots to the pan, and cook for 5 minutes, stirring. Add the flour and cook for 1 more minute.

Gradually add the broth, soy sauce, and wine, then bring to a boil, stirring. Add the cashew nuts and tomato paste, and season well. Pour onto the chicken in the casserole dish. Cover and cook in the oven for 45 minutes.

Place the dumpling ingredients in a bowl. Stir in ½ cup of cold water and knead together to form a dough. Divide into eight pieces and roll these into balls. Uncover the casserole and place the dumplings on top of the chicken mixture. Return to the oven, uncovered, until cooked through, about 15 minutes. Serve.

Chicken Curry with Coconut and Lime

All the different flavors in this exotic-tasting curry marry wonderfully to produce a slightly sweet sauce with a sharp kick provided by the chile. If you think it is too hot, simply reduce the quantity of chile added.

serves 4

I Tbsp vegetable oil	12 oz chicken breast,
2 garlic cloves, minced	boned and skinned
I red onion, halved and	1 1/4 cups chicken broth
sliced	1 1/4 cups coconut milk
1/2 tsp garam masala	2 Tbsp light soy sauce
1/2 tsp ground cumin	Juice and grated zest of
1/2 tsp ground coriander	I lime
1/2 tsp dried lemon grass	2 Tbsp shredded
1/2 tsp mild curry	coconut
powder	2 Tbsp chopped, fresh
1/4 tsp turmeric	cilantro
I red chile, chopped	Cooked rice, to serve

Heat the oil in a large wok or frying pan, then cook the garlic and onion for 5 minutes. Stir in the spices and chile, and cook for 2 minutes. Slice the chicken breast and add, stir-frying for another 5 minutes.

Stir in the broth, coconut milk, soy sauce, and lime juice. Bring to a boil, reduce the heat, and simmer until the chicken is cooked through, about 20 minutes. Sprinkle with grated lime zest and cilantro, and serve with rice.

Orange Turkey Pan-fry

This orange sauce has an almost-caramelized flavor, as the maple syrup and
brown sugar bubble away to perfection, blending with the orange
juice and spices to create a sweet, unique flavor.

serves 4

1 Tbsp vegetable oil	2 Tbsp light soy sauce
4 turkey scallops, skinned	⅔ cup chicken broth
2 garlic cloves, minced	2 Tbsp firmly packed brown sugar
½ tsp ground cumin	2 Tbsp maple syrup
½ tsp ground coriander	1 orange, peeled and sectioned
1 leek, sliced	
1 green bell pepper, cut into strips	1 Tbsp cornstarch
⅔ cup orange juice	Parsley sprigs, to garnish

Heat the oil in a wok or frying pan, and stir-fry the turkey for 10 minutes,
turning until browned.

Add the garlic, spices, leek, and pepper, and stir-fry for 3 to 4 minutes.
Add the orange juice, soy sauce, and chicken broth, and bring to a boil.
Stir in the brown sugar and maple syrup, reduce the heat, and simmer for
about 20 minutes.

Add the orange sections to the mixture. Blend the cornstarch with 2
tablespoons of cold water to form a paste. Add to the sauce and bring to
a boil, stirring until thickened and clear. Cook for 1 minute, and then serve,
garnished with parsley.

Chicken, Apricot and Cilantro Casserole

This recipe uses apricots and herbs to give a slightly Middle Eastern flavor.

serves 4

2 Tbsp vegetable oil	I Tbsp light soy sauce
4 chicken quarters	16 dried apricots
12 baby onions	6 oz asparagus spears
I tsp ground cinnamon	2 Tbsp cornstarch
I tsp ground coriander	2 Tbsp chopped, fresh
I-inch piece fresh	cilantro
gingerroot, shredded	Salt and ground black
2½ cups chicken broth	pepper

Heat the oil in a large wok or frying pan and cook the chicken for 15 minutes, turning until browned. Remove the chicken with a draining spoon, and then place in a large, ovenproof casserole dish. Heat the oven to 350°F. Add the onions, cinnamon, coriander, and ginger to the pan, and cook for 5 minutes. Transfer to the casserole dish, and stir in the broth, soy sauce, and dried apricots. Cover and cook for about 45 minutes.

Remove the casserole from the oven and stir in the trimmed asparagus. Return to the oven until the chicken has cooked through, about 30 minutes. Blend the cornstarch with 2 tablespoons of cold water. Remove the casserole from the oven, and stir in the cornstarch and cilantro. Reheat to thicken, season well, and serve.

Lemon Chicken

This recipe has a piquant sauce, which really gets the taste buds going.

serves 4

8 boned chicken thighs	⅔ cup chicken broth
I Tbsp vegetable oil	Juice and grated zest of
2 Tbsp butter	I lemon
I onion, cut into 16	I Tbsp light soy sauce
pieces	I Tbsp firmly packed
I green bell pepper, cut	brown sugar
into strips	½ cup asparagus spears,
I-inch piece fresh	trimmed
gingerroot, shredded	

Skin the chicken thighs. Heat the oil and butter in a wok, and fry the chicken for 10 minutes. Add the onion, pepper, and ginger, and cook for 5 minutes, stirring. Add the broth, lemon juice, soy sauce, and sugar. Bring to a boil, reduce the heat, and simmer for 15 minutes. Add the asparagus and cook for a further 10 minutes. Sprinkle with the lemon zest, and serve.

Chicken Filo Pie

Filo pastry is easy and convenient to use for both sweet and savory dishes.

serves 6

for the filling

2 Tbsp butter
I leek, sliced
1½ cups chicken breast
meat, chopped
¼ cup all-purpose flour
¼ cup nibbed almonds,
chopped
⅔ cup chicken broth
⅔ cup milk
2 Tbsp light soy sauce

2 oz sun-dried
tomatoes in oil,
drained and sliced
I celery stalk, sliced
½ cup baby corn, sliced
2 Tbsp chopped, fresh
rosemary
Ground black pepper
8 sheets of filo pastry,
thawed
2 Tbsp butter, melted

Melt the butter for the filling in a saucepan, and sauté the leek and chicken
for 5 minutes. Add the flour and cook for I minute. Stir in the almonds,
chicken broth, milk, and soy sauce, and bring to a boil. Add the tomatoes,
celery, corn, and rosemary. Season well.

Heat the oven to 400°F. Place the chicken mixture in a deep-dish pie pan.
Lay a sheet of filo pastry on top of the dish and brush with melted butter.
Repeat once more. Cut the remaining pastry into triangles, and lay on top
in layers, brushing with melted butter. Cook in the oven until golden, about
20 to 25 minutes. Serve.

Stir-fried Duck

A simple dish, which makes good use of a less-frequently-used bird. Duck is perfect when cooked with red-currant jelly and raisins in this risotto-style recipe.

serves 4

10 oz duck breast, skinned	2 Tbsp red-currant jelly
2 Tbsp vegetable oil	2 Tbsp dark soy sauce
1 red onion, sliced	4 oz open-cap mushrooms, peeled and sliced
2 garlic cloves, crushed	
1 tsp Chinese five-spice powder	6 oz arborio rice
1 leek, sliced	1½ pt chicken broth
2 oz raisins	Salt and ground black pepper
1 red bell pepper, cut into thin strips	2 Tbsp chopped, fresh parsley, to garnish

Cut the duck into thin strips. Heat the oil in a wok and stir-fry the duck, onion, garlic, Chinese five-spice powder, and leek for 5 minutes. Add the raisins, pepper, red-currant jelly, soy sauce, mushrooms, and rice, and cook for 2 minutes, stirring.

Pour in the broth, then season and cook until all the liquid has been absorbed, and the rice is fluffy, about 30 minutes. Sprinkle with fresh parsley and serve.

Duck with Bacon and Red Currants

Smoked bacon adds a lot of flavor to recipes. It is fairly strong, and only needs to be used in small quantities. In this dish, it blends perfectly with the duck and red currants.

serves 4	
¾ cup chopped, smoked bacon	3 celery stalks, sliced
1 Tbsp vegetable oil	4 tsp cornstarch
4 half duck breasts	Salt and ground black pepper
2 cups chicken broth	Fresh celery leaves and
4 Tbsp red-currant jelly	red currants to
1½ Tbsp light soy sauce	garnish (optional)

Heat the oven to 350°F. Place the bacon in a shallow, flameproof casserole dish and cook over a moderate heat for 2 to 3 minutes. Add the oil and duck breasts, and cook for a further 5 minutes, turning until browned.

Stir in the broth, red-currant jelly, soy sauce, and celery. Season and bring to a boil. Cover and cook in the oven until the duck is cooked through, about 30 minutes.

Blend the cornstarch with 8 teaspoons of cold water, and stir into the dish. Boil until thickened and clear. Season and serve, garnished with celery and red currants.

Crab Cakes

Serrano peppers are small, very hot peppers. Substitute one jalapeño pepper if necessary. The chiles make these crab cakes quite hot and spicy—so add more or less, depending on your own heat tolerance.

makes 4 crab cakes

Two 6-oz cans white crab meat, with juices from can	1 Tbsp Dijon-style mustard
2 fresh serrano chiles, seeded and minced	1 Tbsp mayonnaise
	1½ tsp light soy sauce
	¼ tsp pepper
1½ Tbsp finely chopped fresh cilantro	1 tsp butter
1 cup bread crumbs	1 tsp corn oil
1 Tbsp finely chopped onion	Salsa, tartar, or cocktail sauce, to serve

Empty the crab meat and juice into a large bowl. Using a fork, mix in the remaining ingredients, stirring thoroughly. Store in the refrigerator for a few hours or overnight, to allow the flavors to blend.

To cook, form into patties—four large or six small. Sauté lightly in the butter and oil, for about 5 to 7 minutes per side. Serve with salsa, tartar, or cocktail sauce.

Scallops with Pecan Crust

This recipe makes a very rich meal. It is best served with a light tossed salad, white wine, and fruit.

serves 4

2 lb large bay scallops
(or sea scallops cut
in half)
1¼ cups ground pecans
(about 2 cups pecan
halves)
1¼ cups fresh bread
crumbs
2 eggs
½ cup flour
2 Tbsp unsalted butter
3 Tbsp oil

for the sauce
2 Tbsp unsalted butter
2 Tbsp flour
1½ cups white wine
1 Tbsp light soy sauce

If the scallops are large, cut them in half. Rinse them with cold water, and then pat them dry with paper towels. The drier they are, the better the coating will stick. Place the ground pecans into a bowl with the bread crumbs, and stir. In a separate bowl, lightly beat the eggs. Put the flour in a third bowl. To coat the scallops, first roll each one in the flour, then dip in the egg, and finally roll in the pecan mixture. Make sure each scallop is thoroughly coated.

Melt the butter and oil in a pan, and sauté the scallops until golden, about 10 minutes. Using a slotted spoon, remove them to a bowl, and keep warm in the oven at 250°F while you make the sauce. Save the pan drippings for the sauce.

For the sauce, add the 2 tablespoons of butter to the pan drippings, and stir until melted. Add the flour, stirring constantly, until a smooth paste is formed. Slowly stir in the wine, a little at a time, mixing well. Add the soy sauce. Simmer for about 5 minutes. It should be thick enough to coat a spoon, but not too thick. Spoon the sauce over the scallops, and serve.

Fish Bites

Use a really "meaty" fish for cubing in this recipe.

serves 4	
10 oz white fish, cubed	for the sauce
2 Tbsp light soy sauce	⅔ cup dry white wine
1 Tbsp lemon juice	5 Tbsp fish broth
2 Tbsp dry white wine	1 Tbsp light soy sauce
½ tsp ground ginger	2 Tbsp ginger wine
1 large zucchini	1 tsp fresh gingerroot,
1 large carrot	shredded
1 Tbsp chopped, fresh	1 Tbsp cornstarch
dill to garnish	2 scallions, chopped

Place the fish in a shallow dish. Mix the soy sauce, lemon juice, white wine, and ginger. Pour over the fish, cover, and marinate for 2 hours.

Meanwhile, using a vegetable peeler, slice the zucchini and carrot lengthwise into thin strips. Blanch the vegetables in boiling water for 1 minute, and then plunge them into cold water. Leave until cold. Soak four wooden skewers in cold water for 30 minutes.

Remove the fish from the marinade, reserving the liquid together with the vegetable strips. Pat the vegetables dry with paper towels. Wrap a piece of zucchini around each fish cube, and then a piece of carrot. Thread four cubes onto each wooden skewer, and brush them with the marinade. Broil for 10 minutes, turning once, and rebrushing with the marinade.

To make the sauce, heat the wine, broth, soy sauce, ginger wine, and ginger in a pan. Bring to a boil. Blend the cornstarch with 2 tablespoons of cold water, and then add to the pan. Return to a boil until thickened, add the scallions and cook for 1 minute. Sprinkle with dill, and then serve.

Barbecued Fish Steaks

Thick fish steaks or fillets, such as cod, salmon, or tuna, are ideal for this recipe.

serves 4

Four 6-oz fish steaks, such as cod, sea bass, salmon, or swordfish
⅔ cup salad oil
⅔ cup red-wine vinegar
I Tbsp firmly packed brown sugar
2 Tbsp light soy sauce
¼ cup dry white wine

I garlic clove, minced
I tsp fennel seeds
I head fennel, trimmed and cut into 8 pieces
2 celery stalks, cut into strips
I red onion, cut into 8 pieces
Grated zest of I lime

Place the fish in a shallow dish. Mix the oil, vinegar, sugar, soy sauce, wine, garlic, and fennel seeds together. Pour over the fish, cover, and marinate for 3 hours.

Remove the fish from the marinade, and place a piece of fish in the center of four squares of foil or wax paper. Divide the vegetables and lime zest between the fish and wrap the foil or paper around to form a parcel. Spoon 2 tablespoons of the marinade over each and seal completely. Cook on hot barbecue coals or broil until cooked through, about 10 to 15 minutes. Serve hot with salad.

Chile Cod and Avocado Salsa

This is a dish with a real Mexican theme, and is fairly hot and spicy.

serves 4

for the avocado salsa	4 cod fillets, skinned
1 large, ripe avocado	1 Tbsp lime juice
2 Tbsp lemon juice	1 onion, chopped
1 tomato, seeded and chopped	1 red bell pepper, chopped
1 onion, finely chopped	2 garlic cloves, minced
Ground black pepper	2 red chiles, chopped
	2 Tbsp light soy sauce
	⅔ cup fish broth
	1 tsp chili powder

To make up the avocado salsa, first halve and seed the avocado, peel, and place in a blender or food processor. Add the lemon juice and blend for 10 seconds until smooth. Transfer to a bowl, adding the tomato and onion. Season well. Cover and chill until required.

Place the cod fillets on 4 large squares of foil. Put the lime juice, onion, red pepper, garlic, chiles, soy sauce, fish broth, and chili powder in a blender and blend for 10 seconds. Spread onto the cod, then wrap the foil around the fish to seal completely. Broil for 10 to 15 minutes and serve with the avocado salsa.

Rice-stuffed Squid

Squid complement this rice-and-olive stuffing, which has a distinctly Greek flavor.

serves 4

1 lb baby squid, prepared and cleaned	¼ cup chestnut mushrooms, diced
¼ cup wild and white rice, mixed	1 Tbsp black, pitted olives, chopped
1¼ cups fish broth	1½ Tbsp capers, chopped
2 Tbsp light soy sauce	1 garlic clove, minced
1 small carrot, diced	Olive oil for brushing
1 Tbsp baby corn	

Chop the squid tentacles and place in a pan. Add the rices, fish broth, soy sauce, carrot, corn, and mushrooms. Cook until the rice is fluffy and the liquid absorbed, about 20 minutes. Add the olives, capers, and garlic to the rice. Use the rice mixture to stuff the squid, securing the open end with a toothpick. Brush the squid with oil and broil for 5 to 6 minutes, turning until cooked. Serve.

Sweet-and-Sour Fish

You can't beat a homemade sweet-and-sour sauce, especially when it coats chunks of tender, fried fish. The cornstarch helps to keep the fish in one piece, and gives it a delicious, crispy coating.

serves 4	
1 lb cod fillet or haddock	2 garlic cloves, minced
1 tsp rice wine or sherry	for the sauce
1 tsp light soy sauce	4 Tbsp firmly packed brown sugar
1 egg, beaten	2 Tbsp vegetable oil
1 cup cornstarch	6 Tbsp garlic wine vinegar
Oil for frying	2 Tbsp dark soy sauce
1 cup canned bamboo shoots, drained and chopped	2 tsp cornstarch
	½ tsp paprika
1 red bell pepper, cut into thin strips	1 tsp sesame oil

Skin the fish and cut the flesh into 1-inch cubes. Mix together the rice wine or sherry, soy sauce, and egg. Stir in the fish. Remove the fish cubes and roll each in the cornstarch to coat.

Heat the oil in a wok until almost smoking, and add the coated fish. Cook until crisp and cooked through, about 5 minutes. Remove from the oil with a slotted spoon, draining on paper towels to remove excess oil. Discard the hot oil, leaving approximately 2 tablespoons in the wok. Add the vegetables and garlic, and stir-fry for 4 minutes. Add the fish and mix well.

Place the sauce ingredients in a pan and stir. Heat gently and pour over the fish mixture. Pour on the sesame oil and serve.

Mixed Fish Casserole

Delicious saffron scones complement a fish dish perfectly. If you do not have saffron, use a pinch of turmeric in its place.

serves 4

8-oz cod fillet	I green pepper, diced
8-oz smoked haddock fillet	Salt and ground black pepper
8-oz trout fillet	
2 Tbsp butter	for the scones
¼ cup all-purpose flour	A few strands of saffron
½ cup dry white wine	or pinch of turmeric
1¼ cups milk	I Tbsp boiling water
2 Tbsp light soy sauce	2 cups self-rising flour
I Tbsp creamed horseradish	½ stick butter
½ cup button mushrooms, sliced	½ cup shredded Cheddar cheese
	⅔ cup milk

Skin and de-bone the fish, cutting the flesh into cubes. Melt the butter in a saucepan, add the flour, and cook for I minute. Remove from the heat, and add the wine and milk, stirring well. Return to the heat and stir in the soy sauce, horseradish, fish, mushrooms, and pepper. Season well and bring to a boil, stirring. Transfer the mixture to a shallow, ovenproof dish.

To make the scones, first place the saffron in the boiling water, and infuse for 10 minutes. Heat the oven to 350°F. Sift the flour into a bowl, and rub in the butter to make crumbly. Stir in the cheese, saffron threads, saffron soaking liquid, and milk. Mix together to form a soft dough. Roll out on a lightly floured surface, and cut into eight equal-sized rounds. Arrange on top of the fish. Bake in the oven until golden, about 45 minutes.

Fish Filo Parcels

These parcels are bursting with shellfish and seafood in a creamy chive sauce.

serves 4

for the filling	8 oz fresh mussels,
2 Tbsp butter	clams, shrimp, and
¼ cup all-purpose flour	squid, shelled and
⅔ cup fish broth	deveined
⅔ cup heavy cream	2 Tbsp chopped, fresh
1 Tbsp light soy sauce	chives
2 tsp lemon juice	Salt and ground black
Few drops of Tabasco	pepper
sauce	
1 lb mixed seafood,	16 sheets filo pastry
thawed if frozen, or	3 Tbsp butter, melted

Melt the butter for the filling in a pan, add the flour, and cook for 1 minute. Remove from the heat and stir in the fish broth, cream, soy sauce, lemon juice, Tabasco sauce to taste, and seafood. Bring to a boil and cook for 5 minutes. Stir in the chives, and season well. Let cool slightly.

Heat the oven to 425°F. Lay four sheets of filo pastry on a work surface. Brush with melted butter and place another sheet on top of each. Repeat twice more. Spoon one quarter of the fish mixture into the center of each pastry sheet. Brush the edges with butter and bring the edges up to enclose the filling. Pull together at the top to close. Brush the parcels with butter and place on a baking sheet. Bake in the oven until golden, about 10 minutes. Serve warm.

Broiled Salmon with Rosemary

Fresh rosemary gives a wonderful aroma and flavor to this dish.

serves 4

Four 4-oz salmon	4 garlic cloves, minced
steaks or 1-lb salmon	2 Tbsp light soy sauce
tail piece, filleted	3 rosemary sprigs
and skinned	6 Tbsp olive oil
	1 Tbsp lime juice
for the marinade	Salt and ground black
1 Tbsp cider vinegar	pepper

Lay the salmon in an ovenproof dish. Mix the liquid marinade ingredients together and pour over the fish. Cover and marinate for 2 hours. Remove the salmon from the marinade and rosemary. Cook under the broiler, turning once or until cooked through, for 10 to 15 minutes, and serve.

Fish Kabobs

Ideal for a summer party, these kabobs make a delicious appetizer or a good alternative to meat.

serves 4

for the marinade	1½ lb cod fillets
3 Tbsp light soy sauce	4 small baking
2 garlic cloves, minced	potatoes, quartered
Few drops of Tabasco	2 red bell peppers,
sauce	sliced into large
2 Tbsp olive oil	squares
1 Tbsp cider vinegar	12 large mushrooms
2 tsp molasses	3 Tbsp olive oil
1 red chile, sliced	Vegetable cooking
⅔ cup fish broth	spray

For the marinade, mix together the soy sauce, garlic, Tabasco sauce, olive oil, cider vinegar, molasses, red chile, and fish broth. Cut the fish into 1½-to-2-inch cubes. Pour the marinade over the fish, and marinate in the refrigerator for several hours or overnight. Precook the potatoes to shorten the barbecuing time. Either use a microwave for 4 minutes on high or boil them, quartered but with skins, until just tender, about 10 to 15 minutes.

To make the kabobs, use either metal or wooden skewers that have been pre-soaked in water for 30 minutes. Then thread the fish cubes, potatoes, peppers, and mushrooms onto the skewers, alternating the ingredients. Brush the vegetables with olive oil.

Spray the broiler with vegetable cooking spray to prevent sticking. Barbecue the kabobs over hot coals, approximately 5 minutes per side.

chapter 4

rice, pasta, and noodles

Spicy Green Rice

There is something very pleasing both to the eye and the palate about a mixture of green vegetables. Perfectly offset by the wild and wholewheat rices, this really is a feast for the eyes.

serves 4

2 Tbsp olive oil	I tsp garam masala
½ cup okra	½ tsp ground cinnamon
I zucchini, cut into thin strips	½ cup nibbed almonds
2 celery stalks, sliced	Generous ½ cup wild rice
½ cup green beans, trimmed	Generous ½ cup wholewheat rice
I green bell pepper, cut into strips	2 Tbsp light soy sauce
I green chile, sliced	2½ cups vegetable broth
I tsp chili powder	5 Tbsp heavy cream
I tsp ground coriander	2 Tbsp chopped, fresh parsley
	Ground black pepper

Heat the olive oil in a wok or frying pan, and sauté the vegetables for 5 minutes. Add the spices, almonds, and rices, and cook for I minute. Stir in the soy sauce and broth, and bring to a boil. Reduce the heat, simmering until all the liquid has been absorbed and the rice is fully cooked, about 30 minutes.

Stir in the cream and half of the parsley, and add seasoning. Transfer to a warmed serving dish, sprinkle with remaining parsley, and serve.

Bean and Pasta Soup

Pasta is ideal as a filler in soups, making them really chunky and wholesome.

serves 4

⅔ cup mixed, dried
beans, soaked
overnight
7½ cups vegetable broth
2 Tbsp olive oil
1 leek, sliced
2 garlic cloves, minced
Scant 1 cup canned,
chopped tomatoes

3 Tbsp light soy sauce
1 cup small pasta shapes
Ground black pepper
¼ cup freshly grated
Parmesan cheese
1 Tbsp chopped, fresh
basil

Drain the soaked beans and rinse them under cold running water. Place in a large saucepan and add the broth. Bring to a boil, then boil vigorously for 10 minutes. Reduce the heat to a simmer, then cook for 1½ hours. Remove half of the beans with a draining spoon, place them in a blender or food processor, and process for 20 seconds. Return to the pan.

In a separate pan, heat the oil, and sauté the leek and garlic for 5 minutes. Add the canned tomatoes and soy sauce, and cook for 2 to 3 minutes. Add the tomato mixture to the pan of beans, with the puréed beans. Stir in the pasta and bring to a boil. Cook until the pasta is done, about 10 minutes. Season with pepper and ladle into a warmed soup tureen. Sprinkle with Parmesan and basil, and serve.

Hot-and-Sour Beef Noodles

Rice noodles are thinner than egg noodles, and have a translucent appearance.

serves 4

12 oz rice noodles
1 Tbsp sesame oil

for the sauce
1 Tbsp groundnut oil
½ lb round steak,
cut into strips
1 red bell pepper, sliced

2 Tbsp dark soy sauce
1 Tbsp chili oil
1 Tbsp Chinese rice
vinegar
4 scallions, sliced
1 tsp firmly packed
brown sugar

Soak the rice noodles in warm water for 25 minutes. Drain and toss in the sesame oil. Meanwhile, heat the groundnut oil in a wok, and stir-fry the beef and red pepper for 7 minutes. Add the soy sauce, chili oil, vinegar, scallions, and sugar. Simmer for 5 minutes. Place the noodles in a warmed serving dish, and spoon on the beef mixture. Serve immediately.

Hot-Pasta Salad

Pasta salads are usually cold, but this colorful recipe really benefits from being eaten warm, as it brings out the flavors in the dressing.

serves 4

for the dressing
2 Tbsp light soy sauce
¼ cup dry white wine
1 Tbsp olive oil
1 Tbsp sesame oil
2 Tbsp balsamic vinegar
2 Tbsp chopped, fresh thyme or parsley
2 tsp wholegrain mustard
1 Tbsp sesame seeds, to garnish
Ground black pepper

8 oz wholewheat pasta shapes
1 tsp salt
1 Tbsp vegetable oil
1 red bell pepper, sliced
1 green bell pepper, sliced
1 yellow bell pepper, sliced
½ cup sugar-snap peas
1 cup small cauliflower flowerets
1 carrot, cut into strips
½ cup sun-dried tomatoes in oil, drained and sliced

Cook the pasta in boiling, salted water until *al dente* ("with bite," or still firm), 8 to 10 minutes. Meanwhile, heat the oil in a large wok or frying pan and stir-fry the peppers, sugar-snap peas, cauliflower, carrot, and tomatoes for 7 minutes. Place the dressing ingredients in a pan and simmer for 2 to 3 minutes.

Drain the pasta and place in a warmed serving dish. Top with the vegetable mixture and pour on the dressing. Sprinkle with sesame seeds, season with pepper, and toss well. Serve immediately.

Chile Chicken Noodles

This recipe has a wonderful, bright-red sauce coating the noodles, making a fiery-looking dish that tastes as hot as it looks!

serves 4

8 oz thin, dried-egg noodles	2 Tbsp light soy sauce
8 oz chicken-breast meat	1 tsp chili oil
Oil for deep frying	2 Tbsp tomato paste
1 Tbsp groundnut oil	2 tsp firmly packed brown sugar
1 tsp Chinese five-spice powder	4 scallions, sliced
1 tsp chili powder	½ cup canned bamboo shoots, drained
2 garlic cloves, minced	1 red chile, chopped

Cook the noodles in boiling water for 5 minutes. Drain and place in a bowl of cold water until required. Slice the chicken breast. Heat the oil for deep frying in a wok until almost smoking. Fry the chicken strips for 3 to 4 minutes. Remove with a draining spoon and drain on paper towels.

Heat the groundnut oil in a wok and cook the spices, garlic, and soy sauce for 30 seconds. Drain the noodles and add to the wok with the chili oil, tomato paste, sugar, scallions, bamboo shoots, and chile. Stir in the chicken, and cook for 4 to 5 minutes. Serve.

Mushroom Pasta

Different varieties of mushrooms add extra interest to this wonderful pasta sauce. Any tagliatelle may be used in the recipe; try using spinach-, tomato-, or garlic-flavored pastas for a change.

serves 4	
8 oz dried or fresh tagliatelle	1 cup wild mushrooms
1 tsp salt	1 cup oyster mushrooms
	2 Tbsp dark soy sauce
for the sauce	⅔ cup vegetable broth
½ stick butter	2 Tbsp chopped, fresh parsley
2 garlic cloves, minced	
1 red onion, quartered	Ground black pepper
1 cup shiitake mushrooms	

Cook the pasta in boiling, salted water for 8 to 10 minutes if dried, and for 5 minutes if fresh, until *al dente* (still firm, or "with bite").

Meanwhile, melt the butter in a saucepan, and sauté the garlic and onion for 5 minutes. Add the mushrooms, soy sauce, and broth, and cook for 4 to 5 minutes.

Drain the pasta and return to the pan. Stir in the mushroom mixture, tossing the pasta to mix thoroughly. Sprinkle with parsley and season well. Spoon into a warmed serving dish and serve immediately.

Noodles with Peanut Sauce

Noodles tossed in a spicy peanut sauce make a quick 'n' tasty satay dish.

serves 4	
½ lb broccoli flowerets	⅔ cup crunchy peanut
I carrot, cut into strips	butter
I leek, sliced	I cup coconut milk
I zucchini, sliced	I Tbsp lime juice
4 scallions, sliced	2 Tbsp light soy sauce
I green chile, sliced	I Tbsp chili sauce
2 Tbsp groundnut oil	I lb egg noodles

Cook all the prepared vegetables in the groundnut oil in a wok or large frying pan for 3 to 4 minutes. Meanwhile, place the peanut butter, coconut milk, lime juice, soy sauce, and chili sauce in a pan. Stir over a low heat until well mixed and hot.

Cook the noodles in boiling water for 2 to 3 minutes. Drain and add to the vegetables. Pour on the peanut sauce and serve immediately.

Pasta and Spinach Soufflé

The three colors of the pasta stand out from the golden color of the soufflé.

serves 4	
4 oz tricolor pasta	3 Tbsp light soy sauce
shapes	Ground black pepper
½ tsp salt	Dash of ground nutmeg
I lb fresh spinach	3 eggs, separated
½ stick butter	I cup Emmenthal
3 Tbsp all-purpose flour	cheese, shredded
Scant I cup milk	I egg white

Grease a 5-cup soufflé dish. Cook the pasta in boiling, salted water for 8 to 10 minutes. Drain and reserve. Blanch the spinach (with stems removed) in boiling water for 2 minutes. Drain well in a sieve, pressing down to remove all the moisture. Heat the oven to 375°F. Melt the butter in a saucepan, stir in the flour, and cook for 1 minute. Remove from the heat, then stir in the milk and soy sauce. Return to the heat and bring to a boil, stirring until thickened. Season with pepper and nutmeg, and cool slightly.

Beat the egg yolks one at a time into the sauce, and add ¾ cup of the cheese. Stir in the drained pasta and spinach. Whisk the egg whites until peaks form, and then fold into the mixture. Spoon into the soufflé dish and sprinkle with the remaining cheese. Stand the dish on a baking sheet. Cook in the oven until risen and set, about 30 minutes. Serve immediately.

Scrambled
Pasta

A complete meal in a pan, this is a perfect brunch or suppertime dish.

serves 4

1 cup small, dried pasta shapes	2 tomatoes, seeded and chopped
½ tsp salt	6 eggs, beaten
1 Tbsp vegetable oil	5 Tbsp milk
4 large, spicy or flavored sausages, such as leek, pepper, herb, or mustard	1 Tbsp light soy sauce
	1 Tbsp butter
	½ cup shredded Cheddar cheese
6 slices smoked bacon, trimmed and chopped	2 Tbsp heavy cream
	Ground black pepper

Cook the pasta in boiling, salted water until *al dente* (still firm), about 10 minutes. Drain well.

Meanwhile, heat the oil in a large wok or frying pan, and cook the sausages for 10 minutes. Remove from the pan, slice, and return to the pan with the chopped bacon and tomatoes. Cook for 5 minutes, stirring, then stir in the drained pasta.

Beat together the eggs, milk, and soy sauce. Add the butter to the pan and pour in the egg mixture. Cook, stirring, for 3 to 4 minutes. Stir in half of the cheese and cook for a further 2 minutes. Stir in the cream, and then spoon the mixture into a warmed serving dish. Sprinkle with remaining cheese, season and serve.

Salmon and Haddock Rice

There are three varieties of rice in this simple recipe, all adding to the dish in their own way. The wild rice adds color, the wholewheat rice a nutty flavor, and the arborio rice a great texture.

serves 4

2 Tbsp vegetable oil	8-oz salmon fillet,
I leek, sliced	skinned and cubed
I garlic clove, minced	8-oz smoked haddock
I tsp dried lemon grass	fillet, skinned and
I tsp curry powder	cubed
¼ tsp turmeric	2 cups fish broth
Generous ⅓ cup	⅔ cup vermouth
wild rice	2 Tbsp light soy sauce
Generous ⅓ cup	Salt and ground black
arborio rice	pepper
Generous ⅓ cup	2 Tbsp chopped, fresh
wholewheat rice	dill

Heat the oil in a large wok or frying pan and sauté the leek and garlic for 3 minutes. Add the lemon grass, curry powder, and turmeric, and cook for a further 2 minutes. Add the three rices and cook for 1 minute, stirring.

Add the salmon and smoked haddock, and then pour in the fish broth, vermouth, and soy sauce. Season and bring to a boil. Reduce the heat to a simmer, and cook until the rice is cooked through and the liquid has been absorbed, about 30 minutes. Sprinkle with chopped dill and serve.

Pasta Gratin

Brightly colored peppers always look spectacular, especially when combined with sun-dried tomatoes, garlic, and olive oil for a true Mediterranean flavor.

serves 4

12 oz dried-pasta bows	2 Tbsp light soy sauce
1 tsp salt	⅔ cup heavy cream
1 Tbsp olive oil	1 Tbsp lemon juice
2 garlic cloves, minced	2 Tbsp chopped, fresh
1 red bell pepper, cut	thyme or parsley
into thin strips	1 egg, beaten
1 green bell pepper, cut	Ground black pepper
into thin strips	¼ cup shredded
3 oz sun-dried	Mozzarella cheese
tomatoes in oil,	
drained and cut	
into strips	

Cook the pasta in boiling, salted water until *al dente* ("with bite," or still somewhat firm), for 8 to 10 minutes. Drain well.

Meanwhile, heat the oil in a wok or frying pan and fry the garlic, peppers, and tomatoes for 5 minutes. Mix the soy sauce, cream, lemon juice, thyme or parsley, and egg. Season. Place the pasta-and-pepper mixture in a shallow, heatproof dish. Pour on the cream mixture.

Sprinkle the dish with the Mozzarella cheese. Cook under the broiler until browned, about 5 minutes. Serve.

Lamb Chops with Tomato Relish

A simple, fresh, tomato-and-herb relish, spiced up with horseradish, is perfect with tender, juicy lamb chops.

serves 4

8 lamb rib chops	1 Tbsp firmly packed
2 Tbsp dark soy sauce	brown sugar
1 Tbsp olive oil	4 tsp red-wine vinegar
1 garlic clove, minced	2 scallions, sliced
2 Tbsp garlic-wine	1 Tbsp horseradish
vinegar	sauce
2 rosemary sprigs	1 Tbsp dark soy sauce
	1 Tbsp chopped, fresh
for the relish	rosemary
4 tomatoes, seeded and	
chopped	

Trim the excess fat from each lamb chop. Scrape the bone with a knife until clean. Place the lamb in a shallow dish. Mix the soy sauce, olive oil, garlic, garlic-wine vinegar, and rosemary together. Pour over the lamb. Cover and marinate for 2 hours.

Meanwhile, place the relish ingredients in a pan and simmer for 5 minutes. Remove the lamb from the marinade and broil for 15 minutes, turning until cooked. Reheat the tomato relish until hot, and then serve immediately with the broiled lamb.

Pork in Filo Parcels

This is a variation on cordon bleu which uses ham and cheese as a topping
for meat, but the flavor is slightly Italian because of the
sun-dried tomatoes and herbs.

serves 4	
4 pork scallops	**½ cup shredded**
2 Tbsp vegetable oil	**Mozzarella cheese**
8 sheets of filo pastry	**I Tbsp chopped, fresh**
2 Tbsp butter, melted	**thyme**
	I oz sun-dried
for the topping	**tomatoes in oil,**
½ cup diced ham	**drained and chopped**
I Tbsp light soy sauce	**Ground black pepper**

Place the pork scallops between two sheets of wax paper and beat with a
meat mallet until ¼-inch thick. Fry in the vegetable oil in a frying pan or
skillet for 10 minutes, turning. Remove from the pan, and drain well on
paper towels to remove excess oil.

Heat the oven to 375°F. Lay four sheets of filo pastry side by side on a
work surface. Brush with butter. Place a further sheet on top of each. Mix
the topping ingredients together. Place a pork scallop in the center of each
sheet of pastry, and top each with a quarter of the ham mixture.

Brush the edges of the pastry with butter and fold around the scallop.
Brush with butter and place on a baking sheet. Bake in the oven until the
parcels are cooked through, about 20 minutes. Serve.

Pan-fried Beef with Peppercorn Sauce

This classic recipe benefits greatly from the addition of soy sauce. Always remember to ignite and extinguish the brandy before returning the pan to the heat.

serves 4

4 sirloin steaks	1 Tbsp vegetable oil
3 Tbsp mixed	2 Tbsp brandy
peppercorns,	1 Tbsp light soy sauce
crushed	⅔ cup heavy cream
2 Tbsp butter	

Trim the steaks of any excess fat. Press the crushed peppercorns onto each side of the steaks. Heat the butter and oil in a wok or frying pan and cook the steaks for 3 minutes on each side. Remove from the pan and keep warm.

Remove the pan from the heat and add the brandy. Ignite and let burn until flame dies down. Stir in the soy sauce and cream. Return the steaks to the pan and heat for a further 3 to 4 minutes. Serve.

Spicy Roast Pork

Tender pork coated in plum glaze and baked with fresh plums looks sensational.
As an alternative to pork tenderloin, use turkey breast.

serves 4

1½ lb pork tenderloin	½ tsp chili powder
2 Tbsp vegetable oil	½ cup plum preserves,
2 Tbsp dark soy sauce	sifted
2 tsp Chinese five-spice	1 Tbsp honey
powder	4 oz plums, seeded and
1 tsp ground cumin	quartered

Heat the oven to 350°F. Trim any excess fat from the meat. Heat the oil in
a roasting pan over a moderate heat. Add the pork and turn to brown all
over. Place the soy sauce, spices, plum preserves, and honey in a saucepan,
and heat until liquid. Brush over the pork, reserving any remaining glaze.

Cook the pork in the oven for 30 minutes. Brush with the remaining glaze.
Return to the oven until cooked through, about 25 to 30 minutes. Arrange
the plum quarters around the pork 10 minutes before the end of cooking
time. Slice and serve with the cooking liquor.

Lamb Hot Pot

The soy sauce really makes the juices in this favorite hot pot extra-special.

serves 4

1½ lb lamb shoulder, boned	2 tsp chopped, fresh thyme
3 Tbsp vegetable oil	Salt and ground black pepper
1 lb leek, sliced	
2 carrots, sliced	2 Tbsp dark soy sauce
1 cup green beans, trimmed	2 cups lamb broth
2 lb potatoes, sliced	⅔ cup dry white wine

Heat the oven to 325°F. Trim the lamb of any excess fat and cut the meat into 1-inch cubes. Heat the oil in a frying pan or wok and sauté the lamb, turning until browned. Layer the lamb, leeks, carrots, beans, and potatoes in a large, ovenproof casserole dish, sprinkling each layer with thyme and seasoning, and reserving enough potato to cover the surface. Mix the soy sauce, broth, and wine together. Pour over the meat and top with a layer of potatoes.

Cover and cook in the oven for 2 hours. Uncover the casserole and increase the temperature to 425°F. Cook the casserole until the potatoes are golden and crisp, about 30 minutes. Serve.

Fruity Burgers

These burgers are succulent, slightly sweet, and have a terrific flavor. Use different dried fruits, such as mango or peach, to vary the flavor.

serves 4

2 cups ground beef	1 Tbsp chopped, fresh cilantro
½ onion, shredded	
2 Tbsp dark soy sauce	1 garlic clove, minced
Salt and ground black pepper	½ tsp ground coriander
	2 Tbsp vegetable oil
½ cup dried apricots, finely chopped	Burger buns, salad, onion slices, and dill pickles, to serve

Place all the ingredients except the oil in a mixing bowl. Mix together well with your hands, and divide into four equal portions. Shape the meat into four flat rounds on a lightly floured board. Heat the oil in a frying pan or wok and cook the burgers, turning once until cooked through, about 10 minutes. Place each burger in a bun with lettuce, onion, and dill pickles, and serve.

Beef Stir-fry

Dried mushrooms are a little bit of a luxury, but well worth purchasing. They add a unique, strong flavor to dishes, and need only be used in small quantities.

serves 4

1 lb lean steak	1 Tbsp vegetable oil
2 Tbsp vegetable oil	4 scallions, cut
3 Tbsp dark soy sauce	lengthwise
1 red chile, chopped	2 celery stalks, sliced
½-inch piece fresh	1 carrot, cut into thin
gingerroot, shredded	strips
2 Tbsp red-wine	1 zucchini, cut into thin
vinegar	strips
2 Tbsp cornstarch	1 cup baby corn, halved
	lengthwise
for the stir-fry	1 cup cauliflower
4 dried Chinese	flowerets
mushrooms	1 Tbsp chili sauce

Cut the beef into thin strips, cutting across the grain. Place in a shallow dish. Mix half of the oil, the soy sauce, chile, ginger, and vinegar together, and pour over the beef. Cover and marinate for 1 hour.

Remove the beef from the marinade with a draining spoon, reserving the marinade. Roll the beef in the cornstarch.

Reconstitute the Chinese mushrooms in boiling water, for 20 minutes. Drain well. Heat the remaining oil in a wok and stir-fry the beef for 4 minutes. Add the scallions, celery, carrot, zucchini, corn, and cauliflower, and stir-fry for a further 4 minutes. Add the reserved marinade to the wok with the chili sauce, stir-fry for 1 minute, and serve.

Lamb with Cranberry Sauce

Cranberries are traditionally associated with turkey, but are just as good with lamb. Use fresh fruit if possible, or frozen cranberries straight from the freezer. If thawed before use, they will disintegrate during cooking.

serves 4

Eight 3-oz lamb loin chops, boned	⅔ cup cranberry juice
2 Tbsp vegetable oil	1 tsp tomato paste
1 cup button mushrooms, halved	¼ cup fresh or frozen cranberries
1¼ cups lamb broth	1 Tbsp chopped, fresh cilantro
2 Tbsp dark soy sauce	1½ Tbsp cornstarch
4 Tbsp cranberry sauce	2 Tbsp cold water

Trim the excess fat from the lamb. Heat the oil in a large frying pan or wok, and fry the lamb for 5 minutes, turning until browned. Add the mushrooms and cook for a further 2 to 3 minutes. Add the broth, soy sauce, cranberry sauce, cranberry juice, and tomato paste. Simmer for 15 minutes, turning the lamb.

Stir in the cranberries and cilantro. Blend the cornstarch with 2 tablespoons of cold water and stir into the pan. Bring to a boil, stirring until thickened and clear. Serve.

Kidneys in Sherry Sauce

Kidneys can be difficult to prepare, so ask your butcher to core them for you.

serves 4

16 shallots	I bay leaf
3 Tbsp butter	3 Tbsp dry sherry
I Tbsp vegetable oil	2 Tbsp dark soy sauce
2 cups chestnut	2 cups lamb broth
mushrooms, halved	A few drops of Tabasco
12 lamb kidneys,	sauce
skinned and cored	Salt and ground black
2 celery stalks, sliced	pepper
2 Tbsp all-purpose flour	Cooked rice, to serve

Halve the shallots. Melt the butter and oil in a large frying pan or wok, and cook the shallots and mushrooms for 3 to 4 minutes. Add the kidneys and celery, and cook for 5 minutes. Stir in the flour and cook for I more minute. Add the bay leaf, sherry, soy sauce, broth, and Tabasco to taste. Cover and simmer until the kidneys are cooked through, about 25 minutes. Serve with freshly cooked rice.

Beef with Pecan Sauce

Serve immediately after the dish is cooked for perfect results.

serves 4

I lb steak,	⅔ cup red wine
cut into strips	I Tbsp soy sauce
I onion, sliced	4 Tbsp lemon juice
3 Tbsp balsamic	Ground black pepper
vinegar	I tsp ground cinnamon
I Tbsp dark soy sauce	1½ cups pecan pieces,
	crushed
for the sauce	I Tbsp all-purpose flour
6 Tbsp olive oil	6 Tbsp heavy cream
3 Tbsp butter	2 Tbsp chopped, fresh
1¼ cups beef broth	cilantro

Place the beef in a shallow dish. Add the onion, vinegar, and soy sauce. Cover and marinate for 2 hours. Heat the oil and butter in a casserole dish. Remove the beef from the marinade, reserving the onion. Cook the beef in the butter, turning until browned all over, about 10 minutes.

Add the reserved onion, broth, wine, soy sauce, lemon juice, seasoning, and cinnamon. Cover and simmer until the beef is tender, about 1½ hours. Mix the pecans and flour together. Stir into the stock with the cream. Simmer for 5 minutes. Garnish with cilantro, and serve.

Lamb Couscous

Couscous is a creamy, nutty alternative to rice. Used extensively in African recipes, it is easy to cook, and steams over the meat sauce for added flavor.

serves 4	
½ cup dried garbanzo beans, soaked overnight, or 1-lb can cooked garbanzo beans, drained	¼ tsp ground cinnamon
	¼ tsp cayenne pepper
	2 red onions, quartered
	2 cilantro sprigs
1 stick butter	1 carrot, cut into chunks
1-lb lamb neck, trimmed of fat, and cubed	4 baby turnips, quartered
1 tsp salt	2½ cups lamb broth
1 tsp ground black pepper	2 Tbsp dark soy sauce
	8 oz couscous
1 tsp ground ginger	2½ cups vegetable broth
¼ tsp turmeric	

Drain the garbanzo beans and place in a large pan. Cover with water and bring to a boil. Boil rapidly for 10 minutes. Drain and rinse.

Melt 6 tablespoons of the butter in a large pan. Add the lamb, salt, pepper, ginger, turmeric, cinnamon, cayenne, onions, cilantro, carrot, and turnips. Cook for 10 minutes, stirring. Add the broth and soy sauce, and stir in the beans. Bring to a boil, cover, and simmer for 1½ hours.

Soak the couscous in the vegetable broth until the water has been absorbed, about 30 minutes. Line a colander with a clean, damp dish cloth, and place the couscous in a mound in the colander. Steam over the lamb for the last 30 minutes of cooking. Stir in 2 tablespoons of melted butter and place on a serving plate. Spoon on the lamb and serve.

sensational salads

Lamb-and-Orange Salad

Hot salads are sensational: the mixture of warm and cold ingredients is a treat.
In this recipe, tender chunks of lamb are sautéed to perfection in soy sauce,
and then served with fennel and fresh orange.

serves 4

1 lb lamb-leg steak
1 Tbsp vegetable oil
1 Tbsp dark soy sauce
1 fennel bulb, sliced
2 oranges, peeled and
sectioned
½ cup pecan halves
4 oz mixed salad leaves,
shredded
½ cup cucumber, sliced
and quartered
Grated rind of 1 orange

for the dressing

3 Tbsp olive oil
3 Tbsp fresh orange
juice
½ tsp prepared
horseradish
Salt and ground black
pepper
2 tsp honey
1 tsp fresh rosemary

Dice the lamb, removing any excess fat. Heat the oil and soy sauce in a
frying pan. Cook the lamb until cooked, 10 minutes. Reserve the lamb and
cooking liquor.

Prepare the remaining ingredients and place in a serving bowl. Remove the
lamb from the pan with a draining spoon and add to the salad.

Mix the dressing ingredients together. Add the cooking liquor from the
pan, stir well, and pour over the salad. Serve.

Sweet Potato Salad

The secret to success with this recipe is to cook the sweet potatoes perfectly. If the potatoes are too mushy, the texture of the salad is not as good. When cooked, a fork inserted into the potato should meet some resistance.

serves 6

2 lb sweet potatoes
½ cup celery, thinly sliced
½ cup green bell pepper, diced
⅔ cup pineapple chunks
½ cup seedless red grapes

¼ cup mayonnaise
1 tsp mild curry powder
½ tsp ground ginger
1 tsp light soy sauce
2 tsp cider vinegar

Boil the sweet potatoes in water until just tender, about 20 minutes. Cool, peel, and cut into 1-inch cubes. Put the potatoes in a bowl with the celery, green bell pepper, pineapple chunks, and grapes.

In a separate bowl, mix the mayonnaise, curry powder, ginger, soy sauce, and vinegar. Gently fold the dressing into the sweet potato mixture. Chill before serving.

Winter Fruit Salad

Exotic fresh fruits make this salad unusual and refreshing. The soy dressing complements the fruit perfectly.

serves 4

1 Tbsp light soy sauce
1 Tbsp cider vinegar
Juice of ½ lime
2 tsp firmly packed brown sugar
8 oz shredded lettuce
10 oz fresh pineapple, peeled, cored, and cut into bite-size pieces

1 mango, peeled, pitted, and cut into chunks
1 green dessert apple, cored and cut into bite-size pieces
¾ cup dates, pitted and chopped
2 Tbsp walnut pieces

Mix the soy sauce, vinegar, lime juice, and sugar together. Arrange the lettuce in a serving bowl.

Add the pineapple, mango, apple, dates, and walnut pieces. Pour the dressing over the top, toss, and serve.

Chinese Vegetable-and-Omelet Salad

Resembling a raw stir-fry, this colorful salad makes use of Asian vegetables. Top with shredded omelet for a special finishing touch.

<table>
<tr><td colspan="2">serves 4</td></tr>
<tr><td>I lb young cabbage</td><td>½ cup salted cashew</td></tr>
<tr><td>Oil for deep frying</td><td>nuts</td></tr>
<tr><td>I tsp salt</td><td></td></tr>
<tr><td>½ tsp ground cinnamon</td><td>for the omelet</td></tr>
<tr><td>2 cups bean sprouts</td><td>2 eggs</td></tr>
<tr><td>4 scallions, halved</td><td>½ tsp Chinese five-spice</td></tr>
<tr><td>lengthwise</td><td>powder</td></tr>
<tr><td>½ cup canned water</td><td></td></tr>
<tr><td>chestnuts, drained</td><td>for the dressing</td></tr>
<tr><td>and chopped</td><td>2 Tbsp light soy sauce</td></tr>
<tr><td>I red bell pepper, sliced</td><td>I Tbsp lime juice</td></tr>
<tr><td>I yellow bell pepper,</td><td>I Tbsp sesame oil</td></tr>
<tr><td>sliced</td><td>½ tsp ground ginger</td></tr>
</table>

Shred the young cabbage. Heat the oil in a wok and deep-fry the cabbage for 4 to 5 minutes. Drain well on paper towels, and sprinkle with salt and cinnamon. Place in a large serving bowl. Top with the bean sprouts, scallions, water chestnuts, peppers, and cashew nuts.

Beat the eggs for the omelet with the Chinese five-spice powder. Heat and oil a 6-inch omelet pan, then pour in the eggs, tilting the pan to coat the base with egg. Cook for 2 minutes until the top is set. Flip over and cook for 2 minutes. Remove and cut into strips. Sprinkle over the vegetables. Mix the dressing ingredients together, pour on, and serve.

Cucumber Salad

Sesame oil has a distinctive taste, so don't substitute any other oil.

serves 4

2 cucumbers (about
1½ lb), peeled
and sliced
2 Tbsp salt
1 Tbsp sesame oil
1½ tsp vegetable oil
4 tsp cider vinegar

1½ tsp light soy sauce
½ tsp sugar
½ tsp mild curry
powder
1 small garlic clove,
minced

Peel the cucumbers and slice very thinly. Sprinkle with the salt and let sit for 3 hours or longer. Rinse the cucumbers very well, squeezing them with your hands to remove liquid. Rinse and squeeze again.

Mix the sesame and vegetable oils, vinegar, soy sauce, sugar, curry powder, and minced garlic. Whisk to blend. Pour over the cucumber, cover, and store in the refrigerator for several hours or overnight before serving.

Chinese Chicken Salad

Soy sauce and ginger make a special dressing for this colorful chicken salad.

serves 4

10 oz cooked chicken,
diced
1 cup canned water
chestnuts, sliced
1 cup alfalfa sprouts
2 tomatoes, seeded
and diced
4 scallions, sliced
1 green pepper, diced
¼ cup unsalted cashew
nuts
1 mango, peeled and
diced

2 heads of Belgian
endive

for the dressing
1 Tbsp light soy sauce
1 tsp ground ginger
2 Tbsp walnut oil
2 Tbsp garlic-wine
vinegar
1 Tbsp honey
1 Tbsp chopped, fresh
parsley
1 tsp lemon juice

Place the chicken in a bowl with the water chestnuts, alfalfa sprouts, tomatoes, scallions, pepper, cashew nuts, and mango. Mix together gently. Arrange the endive around a serving plate and spoon the chicken mixture into the center.

Place all the dressing ingredients in a screwtop jar and shake vigorously to mix. Pour over the salad and serve immediately.

Cilantro Salad

This is a variation on a classic salad, made extra-special by the cheese dressing that is poured over the salad ingredients to add flavor superbly.

serves 4

8-oz head Chinese leaves or bok choy
1 ripe avocado, seeded
1 yellow pepper, diced
½ bunch cilantro, chopped (about ½ oz)
6 scallions, chopped
2 tomatoes, seeded and diced
4 slices bacon, broiled and chopped
1 tsp sesame seeds

for the dressing
¼ cup shredded Parmesan cheese
1 Tbsp sesame oil
4 Tbsp salad oil
1 garlic clove, minced
1 Tbsp honey
2 Tbsp garlic-wine vinegar
¼ tsp Chinese five-spice powder
2 tsp light soy sauce

Wash the Chinese leaves thoroughly and cut into bite-size pieces. Chop the avocado, then add to the leaves with the chopped pepper, cilantro, scallions, tomatoes, bacon, and sesame seeds.

Mix all the dressing ingredients together and pour over the salad. Toss and serve.

Shredded Salad

Celeriac has a strong, fresh aroma and taste, and is a delicious addition to this colorful, simple salad. Serve immediately as celeriac discolors quickly.

serves 4

	for the dressing
1 celeriac	**Juice of 1 lime**
2 zucchinis	**1 Tbsp light soy sauce**
2 carrots	**1 garlic clove, minced**
⅔ cup shredded coconut	**1 Tbsp honey**
Ground black pepper	**Grated zest of 1 lime, to garnish**

Trim the celeriac, peel, and shred finely. Trim and shred the zucchini and carrots, keeping the vegetables separate.

Arrange the individual vegetables and coconut in small mounds on a large serving platter. Season with pepper.

Mix the dressing ingredients together and pour over the vegetables. Garnish the salad with the grated lime zest, and serve immediately.

Carrot, Raisin, and Leek Salad

Caraway seeds are used in this semisweet salad, as they are ideal for both sweet and savory dishes. They have a strong, slightly aniseed flavor.

serves 4

6 large carrots	for the dressing
3 large oranges	⅔ cup fresh orange
⅓ cup raisins	juice
2 leeks	2 Tbsp dark soy sauce
	1 Tbsp maple syrup
	¼ tsp ground nutmeg
	Ground black pepper
	1 tsp caraway seeds

Trim and shred the carrots, then place in a bowl. Peel and section the oranges, and add them to the carrots. Add the raisins. Trim and thinly slice the leeks, stirring into the carrots.

Mix the dressing ingredients together and pour over the salad. Cover and chill until required.

Endive, Bacon and Asparagus Salad

This is a great salad, especially when topped with asparagus and melted cheese.

serves 4

2 heads Belgian endive	1 Tbsp lemon juice
4 slices smoked bacon	2 Tbsp olive oil
12 oz asparagus spears	1 tsp prepared mustard
¼ cup shredded	1 Tbsp garlic-wine
Emmenthal cheese	vinegar
1 Tbsp pine kernels	Ground black pepper
	2 tsp chopped, fresh
for the dressing	thyme
1 Tbsp light soy sauce	

Separate the endive leaves and place them in a shallow, ovenproof dish. Broil the bacon for 10 minutes, turning until crisp; chop roughly. Meanwhile, cook the asparagus in boiling water until tender, for 2 to 3 minutes. Drain well and place on top of the endive leaves. Sprinkle with the bacon, cheese, and pine nuts.

Mix the dressing ingredients together and pour over the salad. Cook under the broiler until the cheese begins to melt, about 3 to 4 minutes. Serve.

Lentil Salad

Lentils make a nutritious and colorful base for this spicy, warm salad.

serves 4

1½ cups red lentils	1 small eggplant, diced
Dash of salt	3 garlic cloves, minced
1 tsp curry powder	½ tsp chili powder
2 cups vegetable broth	¼ tsp turmeric
2 Tbsp vegetable oil	½ tsp ground cumin
1 cup green beans	½ tsp ground coriander
1 cup diced carrots	2 Tbsp light soy sauce
½ cup tomatoes,	2 Tbsp chopped, fresh
seeded and diced	cilantro, to garnish

Wash the lentils, and place them in a large pan with the salt and curry powder. Add the broth and soak for 15 minutes. Bring to a boil, reduce the heat, cover, and simmer for 15 minutes. Turn off the heat and let stand another 5 minutes.

Meanwhile, heat the oil in a frying pan, add the vegetables, garlic, spices, and soy sauce, and stir-fry for 10 minutes. Switch off the heat and let cool. Mix the lentils and vegetables, sprinkle with chopped cilantro, and serve.

Spinach and Noodle Salad

Young spinach leaves should be used for this recipe. The small leaves taste and look terrific with the spicy sauce and noodles.

serves 4

8 oz flat rice noodles

2 Tbsp groundnut oil

8 scallions, sliced

2 garlic cloves, minced

½ tsp star anise, ground

2 tsp chopped, fresh gingerroot

2 Tbsp dark soy sauce

3 oz young spinach leaves, washed

1 Tbsp sesame oil

2 Tbsp chopped, fresh cilantro to garnish

Cook the noodles in boiling water for 4 to 5 minutes. Drain and cool in cold water. Heat the groundnut oil in a wok, and cook half of the scallions, the garlic, star anise, ginger, and soy sauce for 2 minutes, stirring often. Cool completely.

Arrange the spinach in a serving bowl. Drain the noodles and toss into the vegetables. Sprinkle over the sesame oil and place on top of the spinach. Sprinkle with remaining scallions, and serve garnished with fresh cilantro.

vegetable
variations

S w e e t - a n d -
Sour
Vegetables

These vegetables have quite a strongly flavored sauce, and should be served
with plainer meats, fish, or poultry.

serves 4

1 Tbsp olive oil	1 cup mushrooms,
8 oz broccoli flowerets	sliced
½ red onion, thinly	2 Tbsp honey
sliced	1-inch piece gingerroot,
2 zucchinis, sliced	shredded
1 carrot, cut into	2 Tbsp light soy sauce
julienne strips	2 Tbsp cider vinegar
6 cups bean sprouts	

Heat the oil in a large wok or frying pan, and sauté the broccoli for
3 minutes. Stir in the onion, zucchinis, and carrot, and cook for a further
2 to 3 minutes. Add the bean sprouts and mushrooms, and stir-fry for
1 minute.

Mix the honey, ginger, soy sauce, and vinegar together. Pour into the pan,
stir, and cook for 2 minutes. Serve immediately.

Green Peppers and Deep-fried Bean Curd

Quick to prepare, this recipe is best served immediately. If you can't find Chinese mushrooms, use any large mushroom as a substitute.

serves 4

for the sauce	for the dish
1 tsp potato flour	1 Tbsp groundnut or
5 Tbsp mushroom	corn oil
water	2 thin slices fresh
2 Tbsp oyster sauce	gingerroot, peeled
2 tsp light soy sauce	4 large leaves Chinese
2 Tbsp vegetable oil	celery-cabbage,
1 garlic clove, finely	shredded
chopped	1 large green bell
2 scallions, cut into	pepper, seeded and
small sections, white	diced
and green parts	Oil for deep frying
separated	Four 1-inch-square
4 large dried Chinese	cakes bean curd,
mushrooms, soaked,	dried and cut into
squeezed and cut	rectangles
into thin strips	Salt
(water to be	
reserved)	

First make the sauce. Mix the potato flour, mushroom water, oyster sauce, and soy sauce. Heat a wok, add 2 tablespoons of oil, and swirl around. Add the garlic, white scallions, and Chinese mushrooms. Stir for 30 seconds and pour into potato-flour mixture. Reduce heat and continue to stir until the sauce thickens. Remove from heat.

Heat 1 tablespoon of oil in a wok over high heat until smoking. Add the ginger, cabbage, and green pepper. Toss for 30 seconds. Season, reduce heat, and cook, covered, for 2 minutes. Remove and put into a large pan.

Half-fill the wok with oil, turn up heat to 200°F, and lower the bean curd into the oil, one at a time. Fry for 4 minutes, turning over occasionally. Remove with a slotted spoon and drain on paper towels.

Lay the bean curd on the cabbage in the pan and add the green scallions. Heat the sauce and pour over the bean curd. Heat for 2 minutes and serve.

Snow Pea-and-Mushroom Stir-fry

This is a colorful, nutritious, vegetable dish that is quick to cook, and ideal served with broiled meats and fish.

serves 4	
1 cup snow peas	1 cup mushrooms, sliced
1 Tbsp olive oil	2 tsp light soy sauce
1 cup baby corn, halved lengthwise	1 garlic clove, minced
1 cup broccoli flowerets	2 tsp sesame seeds
1 leek, sliced	1 tsp sesame oil

Trim the snow peas. Heat the oil in a large frying pan or wok, and cook the snow peas, corn, broccoli, and leek for 5 minutes.

Stir in the mushrooms, soy sauce, garlic, and sesame seeds, and cook for 3 minutes. Add the sesame oil, stirring, and serve.

Glazed Carrots

This is a very quick recipe for glazed carrots, which are often baked in the oven. As they are quite sweet-tasting, they make a delicious accompaniment to roast meats.

serves 4

I lb baby carrots	2 tsp cornstarch
Juice of 2 small oranges	Grated rind of I orange
2 Tbsp butter	I Tbsp chopped, fresh
2 tsp firmly packed	chives
brown sugar	Ground black pepper
2 tsp dark soy sauce	

Cook the carrots in boiling water for 6 to 7 minutes. Meanwhile, mix the orange juice, butter, sugar, soy sauce, orange rind, and chives in a pan.

Blend the cornstarch with 4 teaspoons of cold water and add to the pan. Bring to a boil, stirring until thickened. Drain the carrots. Place in a serving dish, pour over the sauce, and serve.

Vegetable Spring Rolls

These spring rolls are ideal as part of an Asian meal. Soy sauce gives the vegetables an extra-special flavor.

makes 20 rolls

½ lb fresh bean sprouts	I ½ tsp salt
½ lb young, tender	I tsp sugar
leeks or scallions	I Tbsp light soy sauce
¼ lb carrots	I pack of 20 frozen
¼ lb white mushrooms	spring-roll skins,
Oil for deep-frying	defrosted if frozen

Wash and rinse the bean sprouts and drain them thoroughly. Cut the leeks or scallions, carrots, and mushrooms into thin shreds. Heat 3 to 4 tablespoons of oil in a wok or frying pan, and stir-fry all the vegetables for a few seconds. Add the salt, sugar, and soy sauce, and continue stirring for about I to I½ minutes. Remove and leave to cool a little.

To cook the spring rolls, heat about 6 cups of oil in a wok until it smokes. Reduce the heat for a few minutes to cool the oil a little before adding the spring rolls. Deep-fry 6 to 8 at a time for 3 to 4 minutes, or until golden and crispy. Increase the heat to high again before frying each batch. As each batch is cooked, remove and drain on paper towels. Serve hot immediately.

M u s h r o o m pilaf

Mushroom pilaf is tasty enough to be served alone as a side dish. Or, use it as a base for serving stir-fried entrées.

serves 4	
2 tsp butter	I cup whole-wheat rice
I cup mushrooms,	I cup rosé wine
sliced	I cup chicken broth
½ cup chopped onions	I Tbsp light soy sauce
I garlic clove, minced	2 Tbsp shredded
½ tsp salt	Romano cheese

Heat the butter in a pan, and cook the mushrooms, onions, and garlic until soft but not browned. Add the salt and rice, and sauté for about 5 minutes. Stir in the wine, chicken broth, and soy sauce.

Cover and simmer until the rice is cooked, adding more liquid as necessary. When the rice is ready, stir in the cheese.

Lima Bean-and-Walnut Casserole

Lima beans and walnuts are a great combination, especially when cooked in a mustard sauce and topped with melted cheese.

serves 4

1 lb lima beans, shelled	2 tsp wholegrain
½ tsp salt	mustard
2 Tbsp butter	2 Tbsp light soy sauce
1 onion, cut into	1 cup walnut pieces
16 pieces	Salt and ground black
1 garlic clove, minced	pepper
½ tsp curry powder	½ cup shredded
5 Tbsp vegetable broth	Cheddar cheese

Heat the oven to 350°F. Cook the beans in boiling, salted water for 5 minutes. Drain well. Meanwhile, melt the butter in a frying pan or wok, and cook the onion, garlic, and curry powder for 5 minutes, or until softened. Stir in the broth, mustard, soy sauce, walnuts, seasoning, and drained beans.

Transfer the mixture to a shallow, ovenproof dish and sprinkle with the cheese. Bake in the oven until the cheese has melted, about 30 minutes. Serve at once.

Steamed, Mixed Vegetables

Steaming is one of the healthiest and tastiest methods of cooking vegetables.

serves 4

1 cup cauliflower	¾ cup asparagus spears,
flowerets	trimmed
½ cup snow peas	1 orange bell pepper,
½ cup chestnut	quartered and cut
mushrooms,	into thin strips
quartered	2 Tbsp light soy sauce
1 red onion, cut	1 tsp fish sauce
into 8 pieces	1 tsp dried lemon grass
½ cup canned bamboo	4 tsp lemon juice
shoots, drained	2 tsp fennel seeds

Cut 4 large squares of wax paper. Divide the vegetables equally on the paper squares and scrunch the squares together to form a parcel.

Mix the soy sauce, fish sauce, lemon grass, lemon juice, and fennel seeds. Spoon the mixture on top of the vegetables, and seal the parcels firmly. Cook in a steamer until the vegetables are tender, about 20 minutes.

Deep-fried Mushrooms

Using different varieties of wild and cultivated mushrooms makes this dish very attractive. If possible, marinate the mushrooms for up to 5 hours for a really strong flavor.

serves 4

1 cup oyster mushrooms	2 Tbsp dark soy sauce
1 cup shiitake mushrooms	2 Tbsp chopped, fresh chives
1 cup open-cap mushrooms, peeled and halved	¼ cup all-purpose flour
⅔ cup red wine, such as burgundy	for the batter
	1 egg
2 garlic cloves, minced	⅔ cup water
3 Tbsp red-wine vinegar	1 cup all-purpose flour
	1 Tbsp shredded Parmesan cheese
	Oil for deep-frying

Place all the mushrooms in a shallow dish. Mix the wine, garlic, red-wine vinegar, soy sauce, chives, and flour together. Pour over the mushrooms, cover, and marinate for 2 hours.

Beat the egg and water for the batter together. Sift the flour into a bowl, then stir in the cheese. Make a well in the center and gradually beat in the egg mix to form a smooth batter. Heat the oil in a wok to 375°F.

Remove the mushrooms from the marinade and roll in the flour. Dip into the batter to coat. Deep-fry until golden, about 3 minutes. Drain and pat dry with paper towels. Sprinkle with Parmesan cheese and serve.

Zucchini-and-Sweet-Potato Casserole

The colors of the zucchini and sweet potato make this very visually pleasing. The vegetables are baked in sour cream and topped with melting mozzarella cheese.

serves 4	
I lb sweet potato, sliced	I Tbsp light soy sauce
I lb zucchini, sliced	I Tbsp fresh thyme
I leek, sliced	Salt and ground black pepper
I¼ cups sour cream	½ cup sliced Mozzarella cheese
½ tsp ground allspice	

Cook the sweet potato, zucchini, and leek in a pan of boiling water for 15 minutes. Drain well. Preheat the oven to 325°F. Arrange the zucchini, potato, and leek in a shallow, ovenproof dish. Mix the sour cream, allspice, soy sauce, and thyme together. Pour over the vegetables, and season well with the salt and pepper.

Arrange the cheese on top of the vegetables. Bake in the oven until golden, about 30 minutes.

Spicy Beans

These beans have a rich, caramel flavor, due to the molasses and brown sugar. They are quite filling, and almost a meal in themselves.

serves 4	
I⅓ cups dried beans, soaked overnight	2 Tbsp tomato paste
I tsp salt	14-oz can chopped tomatoes
I onion, halved and sliced	2 Tbsp firmly packed brown sugar
I green bell pepper, cut into strips	I Tbsp molasses
½ cup diced, cooked smoked ham	2 Tbsp dark soy sauce
½ cup sliced spicy sausage	⅔ cup vegetable broth
	I Tbsp cider vinegar
	I green chile, chopped
	I tsp paprika

Drain and rinse the beans, then place them in a pan of salted water. Bring to a boil, and boil rapidly for 10 minutes. Remove any foam with a slotted spoon. Drain well. Heat the oven to 350°F. Place the beans in a casserole dish. Add the onion, pepper, ham, and sausage. Mix the tomato paste, tomatoes, brown sugar, molasses, soy sauce, broth, vinegar, chile, and paprika. Pour over the bean mix, stir, and cover. Cook in the oven for 50 minutes.

Sweet Potato Muffins

These sweet, moist muffins are good either plain or served with honey.

makes about 12	
1 lb sweet potatoes, cooked, peeled, and mashed	2 eggs
	1 Tbsp baking powder
1 stick butter	1 Tbsp light soy sauce
½ cup brown sugar	¼ cup milk
	1½ cups flour

Boil the sweet potato in a pan of water until soft, about 20 minutes. Peel and mash. Heat the oven to 375°F. Cream the butter and brown sugar together. Add the mashed sweet potato, eggs, baking powder, and soy sauce. Finally, stir in the milk and flour, and mix thoroughly.

Stir-fried Zucchini with Sesame Seeds

Soy sauce brings out the flavor of zucchini, and the sesame seeds add crunch.

serves 4	
4 large zucchinis (about 2 cups when sliced)	4 tsp light soy sauce
	½ tsp dill weed
2 tsp olive oil	2 tsp sesame seeds

Wash the zucchini and then slice into ⅛- to ¼-inch rounds. Heat the oil in a nonstick pan over medium heat, then add the zucchini. Sprinkle the soy sauce and dill weed over the top, and sauté for 3 to 4 minutes until the zucchini begins to wilt. Add the sesame seeds and continue cooking until the zucchini starts to brown, about 3 or 4 minutes. Serve immediately.